# HYSTERICAL JOKES FOR MINECRAFTERS

## BLOCKS, BOXES, BLASTS, AND BLOW-OUTS

BRIAN BOONE

Illustrations by Amanda Brack

Sky Pony Press
New York

Sky Pony Press books may be purchased in bulk at special discounts for sales promotion, corporate gifts, fund-raising, or educational purposes. Special editions can also be created to specifications. For details, contact the Special Sales Department, Sky Pony Press, 307 West 36th Street, 11th Floor, New York, NY 10018 or info@skyhorsepublishing.com.

Sky Pony® is a registered trademark of Skyhorse Publishing, Inc.®, a Delaware corporation.

Visit our website at www.skyponypress.com.

10 9 8 7 6 5 4

Library of Congress Cataloging-in-Publication Data is available on file.

Cover design by Brian Peterson
Cover illustration credit Hollan Publishing, Inc.
Cover and interior illustrations by Amanda Brack

Print ISBN: 978-1-5107-1882-1
Ebook ISBN: 978-1-5107-1885-2

Printed in the United States of America

# CONTENTS

# INTRODUCTION

Hey, we heard you dig Minecraft, so we tooled around for a while, shoveled a few things around, and *BOOM*—we came up with this joke book just for you. Thanks for picking up *Hysterical Jokes for Minecrafters: Blocks, Boxes, Blasts & Blow-Outs*.

We've taken a long look at the Minecraft world to find the funny side of all of the ore-seeking and creeper-wrecking. Minecraft may look dark and serious, but trust us: There's a lot of humor to be mined. (*Ha*!) Whether you're a longtime Minecrafter or a new kid on the "block," we think you'll have an explosively good time reading and telling your friends these jokes, and this book will make a great tool in your arsenal of tools against the real hostile mobs: people with no sense of humor!

So start chipping away at these jokes. They're diamonds in the rough! Comedy gold! They'll really help you get the lead out!

# CHAPTER 1

## BLOCK PARTY

**Q: Where does Steve's best friend live?**

A: Just around the block.

■

**Q: Have you seen the new Minecraft movie?**

A: You haven't? It's a blockbuster!

■

**Q: Where does Steve get his taxes done?**

A: H&R Block.

**Q: What do zombies and skeletons need in the morning?**

A: Sunblock.

**Q: Why are there no cars in Minecraft?**

A: Because the streets are blocked off.

**Q: How do you block the sun?**
A: Sunblock.

■

**Q: What's the most popular playground game in Minecraft?**
A: Four Square.

■

**Q: How come Steve doesn't get invited to parties?**
A: He's too square.

■

**Q: Why did Steve quit social media?**
A: He kept getting blocked.

■

**Q: Why is everything in Minecraft made of blocks?**
A: Because it's hard to stack up spheres.

■

**Q: Why was Steve a terrible author?**
A: Writer's block!

**Q: How does Steve defend his house?**

A: He blocks the door.

**Q: What's the top social network for Minecrafters?**

A: Faceblock.

**Q: How does a Minecrafter get exercise?**
A: They run around the block.

■

**Q: Why did Steve put wood blocks on his bed?**
A: So he could sleep like a log.

■

**Q: Did you hear about the farmer who only planted blocks of hay?**
A: He thought he could grow straw-berries.

■

**Q: How do you stop a hostile mob from attacking you?**
A: You block their path.

■

**Q: What did Minecraft Christopher Columbus do?**
A: He proved the world was square.

■

**Q: What happens when a chicken lays a square egg?**
A: It says "ouch!"

**Q: Why would Charlie Brown do well in Minecraft?**
A: Because he's a blockhead!

■

**Q: Who's a Minecrafter's favorite composer?**
A: Johann Sebastian Block.

■

**Q: What is Notch's only character flaw?**
A: He can't think outside the blocks.

■

**Q: How do you know if your Minecraft character is sick?**
A: Its nose is blocked.

■

**Q: What did the dirt block say to Steve?**
A: "Why are you always picking on me?"

■

**Q: How much dirt is in a hole that measures two blocks by three blocks by four blocks?**
A: There is no dirt in a hole! (At least not anymore.)

**Q: What's the difference between the law and an ice block?**

A: One is justice and the other is just ice.

■

**Q: How is playing Minecraft like DNA?**

A: It's all about the building blocks of life.

■

**Q: Where's the worst place to get stuck in Minecraft?**

A: In a 1-by-1 hole with another person.

■

**Q: What do chickens in Minecraft say?**

A: "Block, block, block!"

■

**Q: What would a rooster in Minecraft say?**

A: Block-a-doodle-doo!

■

**Q: Where do most Minecrafters live?**

A: Apartment blocks.

**Q: What do you get when you cross LEGO with death?**
A: Minecraft.

■

**Q: What did the Minecraft character say to the barber?**
A: "Give me a flattop."

**Q: How do you prevent water from flooding your house in Minecraft?**
A: Put up a fence!

**Q: What do a toddler and a Minecrafter have in common?**
A: They both love to play with blocks.

■

**Q: What do Minecrafters call Tetris?**
A: Primitive Minecraft.

■

**Q: What's the most popular TV game show in Minecraft?**
A: Overworld Squares.

■

**Q: To what cartoon character does Steve most relate?**
A: SpongeBob SquarePants.

■

**Q: What was Steve's favorite TV show when he was little?**
A: Bob the Builder.

■

**Q: Why do parents love Minecraft?**
A: Because it's all about character building!

**Q: Why can't you play *Scrabble* with a Minecrafter?**

A: Because they take all the tiles.

■

**Q: What board game makes a Minecrafter cringe?**

A: *Jenga*.

■

**Q: How are crops in Minecraft like a math book?**

A: They both have square roots.

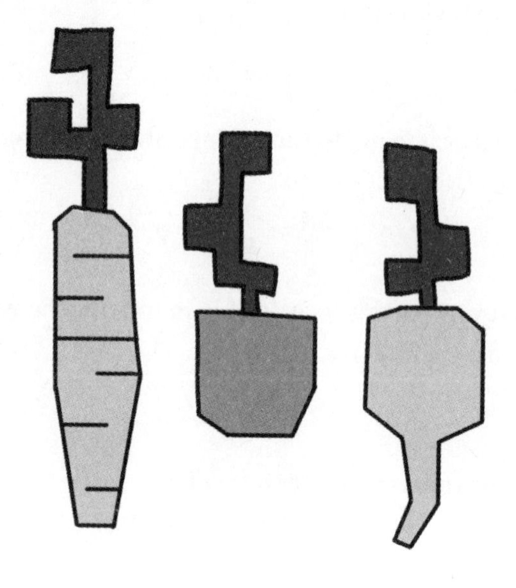

**Q: What kind of parties do Minecrafters throw?**
A: Block parties.

■

**Q: How did Steve tell his friends he was going out to mine for a while?**
A: He left a Note Block.

■

**Q: What's wet, full of holes, but doesn't leak?**
A: A Sponge Block.

■

**Q: What is every trade in Minecraft, ultimately?**
A: A square deal.

■

**Q: What can you send a Minecrafter who's far away and feeling lonely?**
A: A square package.

**Q: If the Rolling Stones existed in the world of Minecraft, who would be their lead singer?**
A: Brick Jagger.

■

**Q: What's a pixel?**
A: The building block of life!

■

**Q: When is a Minecraft diamond not a diamond?**
A: When it's Cubic Zirconia.

■

**Q: Who's a Minecrafter's favorite rapper?**
A: Ice Cube.

■

**Q: Where do Minecrafters go to invest their loot?**
A: The block market.

■

**Mario:** I destroy every block I see!
**Steve:** You *what?!*

**Q: What did Steve say to the Villager?**

A: "Haven't I seen you *a-square* these parts?"

■

**Q: What do the number thirty-six and a Minecraft block have in common?**

A: They're both perfect squares.

■

**Q: What's the best way to chill out in Minecraft?**

A: With a bucket of Ice Blocks.

■

**Q: What's a Minecrafter's favorite kind of fish?**

A: Walleye.

■

**Q: What kind of blocks would you find near an angry creeper?**

A: Cinder blocks.

■

**Q: What's the difference between New York City and Minecraft?**

A: One has the great Times Square and the other is a great square time!

**Q: Who's the president of Minecraft?**

A: Brick Obama.

■

**Q: What does Steve keep in an old drawer?**

A: Brick-a-brack.

■

**Q: How did Steve propose to Alex?**

A: He put a rock on her finger.

**Q: What do you get if you cross a chicken and some clay blocks.**

A: A brick-layer.

■

**Q: What do Minecrafters tell their kids to do when they're bored?**

A: "Go do something constructive!"

■

**Q: What's an insult in the real world but a compliment in Minecraft?**

A: "You're such a square!"

■

**Q: What structure do you build to store your shovel?**

A: A shovel hovel.

■

**Q: What do Minecrafters call LEGO enthusiasts?**

A: Un-imaginative!

**Q: Why doesn't Steve like *Tetris*?**

A: He thinks it's a little too two-dimensional.

■

**Q: What's the difference between a boxer and a Minecrafter?**

A: One would punch and the other would punch wood.

■

**Q: What's the hardest part about falling off of a high tower?**

A: The ground!

■

**Q: What do you call horses that linger near your structure?**

A: Neigh-bors.

■

**Q: What's the most difficult puzzle to solve in Minecraft?**

A: A Rubik's Magma Cube.

# CHAPTER 2

## THINKING INSIDE THE BOX

**Q: What's a Minecrafter's favorite sport?**

A: Boxing.

■

**Q: How do you distract a Minecrafter?**

A: Put him in a room full of empty cardboard boxes.

■

**Q: What's Steve's favorite kind of dog?**

A: A boxer.

■

**Q: What did Steve get Alex for Valentine's Day?**

A: A box of chocolates.

**Q: What's Steve's favorite Greek myth?**
A: The story of Pandora's Box.

■

**Q: Where does Steve rent movies?**
A: Redbox.

■

**Q: How does Steve keep up his strength?**
A: He eats three square meals a day.

■

**Q: Does a Minecrafter like Christmas?**
A: Sure, but they prefer Boxing Day.

■

**Q: What does an Ocelot need to use in *Minecraft*?**
A: The litterbox.

**Q: What's a Minecrafter's favorite part of a city?**
A: The Town Square.

■

**Q: What's a good name for rookie Minecrafters?**
A: Cube Noobs.

■

**Q: What's the most popular video game system in *Minecraft*?**
A: Game Cube.

■

**Q: Where does Steve go to get his cart serviced?**
A: Jiffy Cube.

■

**Q: What service does Steve use to get a ride back to his house?**
A: Cuber.

**Q: What's a Minecrafter's favorite form of art?**

A: Cubism.

**Q: What's the difference between Steve's heart and his diamonds?**

A: One gets stored in his chest, and the other is stored in his chest!

**Q: What toy always surprises a Minecrafter?**
A: A Jack-in-the-Box.

■

**Q: Why didn't the miner like staying inside his own houses?**
A: He was claus-tro-pho-brick.

■

**Q: What would a surfer call Minecraft?**
A: "Totally cubular!"

■

**Q: What's the most popular ride at the Minecraft carnival?**
A: The Merry-Go-Cube.

■

**Q: What's a Minecrafter's favorite kind of dancing?**
A: Square dancing.

**Q: How does Steve measure his boot size?**

A: In square feet.

■

**Q: Why didn't Steve like the Cobblestone Wall?**

A: Because it was a moss!

■

**Q: What's an inexpensive gift you can give a Minecrafter?**

A: An empty box. You can tell them it's an Air Block.

■

**Q: Why did Steve install plates around his house?**

A: He was being pressured.

■

**Q: Where does Steve keep all of his love notes from Alex?**

A: In a heart-shaped box.

**Q: What animal should really be in Minecraft?**

A: The box turtle.

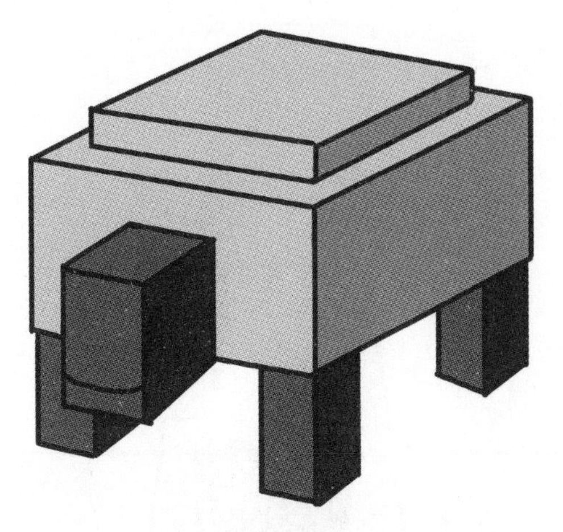

**Q: How many blocks do you need to make a gallon in the Nether?**

A: Four quartz!

**Q: Why didn't Steve like his tiny house?**

A: He felt boxed in.

**Q: What's a Minecrafter's favorite part of a pizza?**

A: The box.

**Q: What did Steve call a block he didn't use anymore?**

A: An ex-box.

**Q: Where can you get all the Minecraft updates in one place?**
A: A box set.

■

**Q: Where would you put items and weapons you don't need anymore?**
A: In the litter box.

■

**Q: What happens after your character dies in Minecraft?**
A: You're back to square one.

■

**Q: What kind of box is the most valuable in Minecraft?**
A: A full toolbox!

■

**Q: What kind of box should you never put near lava?**
A: A matchbox.

**Q: What's a Minecrafter's dream car?**
A: A Porsche Boxster.

■

**Q: Where did Steve put all of his extra diamonds?**
A: In a jewelry box.

■

**Q: Where did Steve put all of his extra cake?**
A: In his lunch box.

■

**Q: Where does all the music in Minecraft come from?**
A: A music box!

■

**Q: What happened when Steve accidentally ate a bunch of rocks?**
A: His voice sounded all gravelly.

**Q: Who's a Minecrafter's favorite comedian?**
A: Chris Rock.

■

**Q: Who's a Minecrafter's favorite actress?**
A: Emma Stone.

■

**Q: Why didn't Steve put any windows in his house?**
A: He couldn't take the pane.

■

**Q: Did you hear the one about the roof Steve built?**
A: Never mind, it's probably over your head.

■

**Q: What sickness did Steve get after building his roof?**
A: Shingles.

**Q: Which hostile mob can jump higher than a house?**
A: All of them. Houses can't jump.

■

**Q: Where's the best place in your house to put your porch?**
A: On the outside.

■

**Q: What did the floor planks say to the ceiling?**
A: "I look up to you."

■

**Q: What can you put in the dirt to make it lighter?**
A: A hole.

■

**Q: Which building has the most stories?**
A: The library.

**Q: What's a Minecrafter's favorite part of rap music?**

A: The beat-boxing.

**Q: How do stairs travel?**

A: By flight.

■

**Q: Where does Steve get everything to furnish a house?**

A: Bed, Blocks, and Beyond.

**Q: What kind of stone can you get at the Overworld Library?**
A: Redstone.

■

**Q: What kind of Minecraft construction weighs the least?**
A: A light-house.

■

**Q: Steve was so cold he stood in the corner of his house. Why?**
A: Because it was 90 degrees there.

■

**Q: Why are Minecrafters terrible at math?**
A: Because every time they see a number they cube it.

■

**Q: What do you call a Minecraft structure with holes in the walls?**
A: A house on the brick of collapse.

**Q: What are the ABC's of Minecraft?**
A: Always Be Crafting.

■

**Q: What did Steve call the multi-story pig pen he built?**
A: A sty-scraper.

**Minecraft:** Be there *and* be square!

# CHAPTER THREE

## DYN-O-MITE!

**Q: What happened to Steve's house after a fireplace accident?**

A: It went down in a blaze of glory.

■

**Q: What happened when Steve tried to get up in front of an audience and tell some Minecraft jokes?**

A: He bombed.

■

**Q: Why is Minecraft so fun?**

A: Because it's da bomb!

**Q: What do you get if you cross a spawn egg with TNT?**

A: An egg-splosion.

**Q: What happened when Steve read a giant book of philosophy?**

A: It blew his mind.

**Q: Why did Steve blow up his own house with TNT?**

A: He got caught up in the heat of the moment.

**Q: Where do things go when you blow them up with TNT?**
A: To smithereens!

■

**Q: Where do things go when creepers blow them up?**
A: Kingdom Come!

■

**Q: Where did the creeper go after the explosion?**
A: Everywhere!

■

**Q: What's the difference between TNT and lava?**
A: One blows and one glows.

■

**Q: What's a great Halloween game in Minecraft?**
A: Bombing for apples.

■

**Q: What's the difference between a creeper and a Nether resident?**
A: One is a blast and one is ghast.

**Q: Which biome is the most explosive?**

A: Mush-a-BOOM!

■

**Q: How do you get a pig to fly?**

A: Set off some TNT nearby.

**Q: What do you get when you cross a cow with TNT?**

A: Evaporated milk.

**Q: How is NASA like Minecraft?**

A: Both are the most fun when something is blasting off.

■

**Q: What happened to the man who tried to reform a creeper?**

A: The project blew up in his face.

■

**Q: What goes "*Ha Ha BOOM*"?**

A: A creeper who heard a good joke.

■

**Q: What did the creeper say to Steve?**

A: Nothing! It just blew up!

■

**Q: What goes best with Minecraft cookies?**

A: Tea-NT

■

**Q: What's black and white but red all over?**

A: TNT.

**Q: What did the snow golem get when he saw a structure explode?**
A: Cold!

■

**Q: Why was the creeper full of regret?**
A: Because he exploded far away from any structure.

■

**Q: Did you hear about the creeper's birthday party?**
A: It was a blowout!

■

**Q: What sound do you get when TNT falls onto a cow?**
A: Cow-boom!

■

**Q: What would you get if you crossed a creeper and a primate?**
A: A ba-boom.

■

**Q: Who's a creeper's favorite pioneer?**
A: Daniel Boom.

**Q: Why don't creepers have many friends?**

A: They have explosive tempers.

■

**Q: What's a creeper's favorite toy?**

A: A BOOMerang.

■

**Q: Why do creepers ruin birthday parties?**

A: Because they blow up all the balloons.

■

**Q: What do you call a competition between two creepers?**

A: A blast-off.

■

**Q: What happened when a creeper didn't sneak up and kill a player?**

A: He blew his chance.

■

**Q: What do you get when a creeper visits a wooden house?**

A: Sawdust!

**Q: What do you get when you cross an angry creeper and a cow?**

A: Powdered milk.

■

**Q: What should you get from a creeper?**

A: As far away as possible.

■

**Q: What's green and has a suitcase?**

A: A creeper on vacation.

**Q: What's the biggest creeper river?**
A: The Hississippi.

■

**Q: What happens when you put ten creepers into a room together?**
A: An explosively good time.

■

**Q: What award did a creeper win in his high school yearbook?**
A: "Most Explosive."

**Q: What's the most popular haircut in Minecraft?**
A: A blowout.

■

**Q: What do you get if you cross TNT with a chicken?**
A: An eggs-plosion.

■

**Q: Is it necessary to blow up a vast amount of TNT all at once?**
A: No, you only need to light a fuse.

■

**Q: What did one torch say to the other torch?**
A: Going out tonight?

■

**Q: What real-life event sounds like a day of Minecrafting gone bad?**
A: Burning Man.

# CHAPTER FOUR

## THE RIGHT TOOL FOR THE JOB

**Q: What tool is almost completely see-through?**

A: Shears!

■

**Q: Why did Steve run around while he was digging?**

A: He wanted to get the lead out.

■

**Q: What is a chicken's favorite Minecraft tool?**

A: Clock-clock-clock!

■

**Q: When should you use shears?**

A: When things are getting really shearious.

**Q: How do miners pick their noses?**

A: With a pickaxe.

**Q: What do cobblestone and your nose have in common?**

A: They're both hand-picked!

**Q: What did the miner sleep on when he couldn't find a bed?**

A: Bedrock.

■

**Q: How did Steve feel after a day of unsuccessful mining?**

A: Ore-ful!

■

**Q: Why did Steve go after a skeleton with a pickaxe?**

A: He had a bone to pick with him.

■

**Q: Why should you bring iron and gold into a boat?**

A: Because you're going to need ores.

■

**Q: How do you freshen your breath in Minecraft?**

A: With breath flints.

■

**Q: How do you give a Minecrafter a present?**

A: Put a bow on it.

**Q: Why couldn't the Minecrafter get to the diamonds?**
A: Something was blocking his way.

■

**Q: Why couldn't the Minecrafter think of a way to get more ore?**
A: He just had a mental block.

■

**Q: Why did the miner choose to mine alone, away from the other miners?**
A: They were picking on him.

■

**Q: What's the most popular snack in Overland?**
A: Carrot-on-a-stick.

■

**Q: Where does Steve keep his secrets?**
A: Close to the chest.

**Q: Why did Steve go get a load of water?**
A: Because it was on his bucket list.

■

**Q: What did Steve say to the diamond block?**
A: "I dig you."

■

**Q: How does Steve chop down a tree with his bare hands?**
A: How wood we know?

■

**Q: What's the best place to shear a sheep?**
A: At the baa-baa shop.

■

**Q: How do you confuse a Minecrafter?**
A: Put two shovels in a chest and tell him to take his pick!

**Q: What's the best armor you can use to protect a horse in Minecraft?**

A: Horse, of course.

■

**Q: What's the funniest item to collect in Minecraft?**

A: Laugh-is Lazuli.

■

**Q: How would you politely remove a stone block?**

A: With a pick-ask.

■

**Q: What's the first thing you do if you're going to chop wood in Minecraft?**

A: Pickaxe.

■

**Q: What does Steve wear to smell nice?**

A: Axe Body Spray.

**Q: What instrument does Alex play in the Minecraft band?**

A: Axe-o-phone.

**Q: What kind of berry farms are in Minecraft?**
A: U-Pick.

■

**Q: What did the sheep say after Steve took its wool?**
A: "Sheariously?!"

■

**Q: What did Steve say when he lost his pickaxe?**
A: "Where's my pickaxe?"

■

**Q: Why couldn't Steve afford any bread?**
A: He was all out of butter.

■

**Q: What did Steve say when someone else took his diamonds?**
A: "You mined?"

**Q: How does Alex get a hold of Steve?**
A: She sends him a texture message.

■

**Q: What Steve say when he discovered diamonds?**
A: "Ore-some!"

■

**Q: Why did Steve cut down the tree?**
A: He didn't mean to—it was an axe-ident.

■

**Q: When should you place wood stairs near brick stairs?**
A: If you're having a stairing contest.

■

**Q: How did the Diamond Sword win its argument with Steve?**
A: It made some good points.

**Q: What is Santa Claus's favorite tool to use in Minecraft?**

A: The hoe, hoe, hoe!

■

**Q: What's Steve's favorite kind of music?**

A: Heavy metal.

■

**Q: Why can't you start looking for ore right away?**

A: You must axe!

■

**Q: Did you hear that Steve hurt himself hiding his treasure?**

A: Yep, he had chest pains.

■

**Q: How did they catch the redstone thief?**

A: He was red-handed.

**Q: How did Steve feel when he spent hours mining only to find nothing but coal?**

A: Shafted.

■

**Q: Why did the sailor bring iron and gold into his boat?**

A: He needed oars.

■

**Q: When is the best time to make Minecraft eggs?**

A: At spawn.

■

**Q: What do you call a miner with a shovel in his head?**

A: Doug.

■

**Q: What do you call a miner with an axe in his head?**

A: Axel.

**Q: What's the biggest fad in Minecraft?**
A: Planking.

■

**Q: What's better than a stack of diamonds?**
A: Two stacks of diamonds.

■

**Q: Why did Steve jump across the lava pool?**
A: Because there were ten diamond blocks on the other side.

■

**Q: What did Steve's cobblestone house turn into after Steve got addicted to Minecraft?**
A: Mossy cobblestone.

■

**Q: Why was Steve's fresh obsidian worthless?**
A: He couldn't get it out of the bucket!

■

**Q: Why did Steve wear rocks for shoes?**
A: He thought it was cobbler-stone.

**Q: Why did Notch add pistons to Minecraft?**
A: People were pushing him to add them.

■

**Q: After boxing, what's the second most popular sport in Minecraft?**
A: Fencing.

■

**Q: When's the best time of day to create new Minecraft creatures?**
A: Spawn-set.

■

**Q: What game can you play completely mentally?**
A: Mind-craft.

■

**Q: What's so nice about cobblestone?**
A: It's handpicked.

■

**Q: What did one wall say to the other wall?**
A: "I'll meet you at the corner!"

**Q: How do you confuse a Minecrafter?**

A: Give him a shovel, an axe, and a hoe and tell him to take a pick.

■

**Q: How many Minecrafters does it take to change a light bulb?**

A: None. Notch hasn't put them in the game yet.

■

**Q: Where do rich Minecrafters live?**

A: Emerald City.

■

**Q: What's a day that Steve spends mining?**

A: An ore-dinary day.

■

**Q: What do you call it when you find iron right after your pickaxe breaks?**

A: Ironic.

**Q: What's it called when Steve's trapped at the bottom of his mine?**

A: Stuck between a bed-rock and a hard place.

■

**Q: What does Steve talk about when he's fishing?**

A: Reel talk.

**Q: Why won't Steve explore really deep holes?**
A: Because they're the pits!

■

**Q: What's Steve's favorite reference book?**
A: The dig-tionary.

■

**Q: Where's the best place to keep your gold and emeralds in the Ice Biome?**
A: A snow bank.

■

**Q: How does Steve make a house in the Ice Biome?**
A: Igloos it together.

■

**Q: How is a cart like a jukebox?**
A: One is good for a roll in rock, and other is good for rock n' roll.

**Q: What's the best way to catch a fish in Minecraft?**
A: Wait for it to rain.

■

**Q: What did the leggings, helmet, and chest plate say to the boots?**
A: "You complete me!"

■

**Q: What did the villager do to prevent theft at his farm?**
A: He put up a "CROP" sign.

■

**Q: What do creepers use to cut things?**
A: Hissors.

■

**Q: What did everyone yell when the diamond walked into the room?**
A: "Mine!"

**Q: What's the difference between Steve as a child and Steve now?**
A: Back then he was a minor and now he's a miner.

■

**Q: What do Minecrafters use to search the Internet?**
A: Axe Jeeves.

■

**Q: What's the only thing harder than diamonds?**
A: A diamond pickaxe.

■

**Q: What's green and makes holes?**
A: A drill pickle.

■

**Q: What's a song about a Minecraft cart called?**
A: A cart-tune.

**Q: Where's the best city to make new tools?**
A: Anville.

■

**Q: Why did Steve eat a torch?**
A: He was in the mood for something light.

■

**Q: Which weighs more: a chest full of gold or a chest full of feathers?**
A: In Minecraft, they weigh the same!

■

**Q: Why did Steve pour a bucket of water on the ground?**
A: He wanted to make a big splash.

■

**Q: Which Minecraft tool is almost see-through?**
A: Shears.

**Q: What kind of structure could you build using only shears?**

A: A shear-amid.

■

**Q: What should you always remember to wear in the Tundra Biome?**

A: Your tundra-wear!

■

**Q: What does Old Steve use to walk?**

A: Sugar cane.

■

**Q: What did Steve name his fishing pole?**

A: Rod.

■

**Q: What did Steve do after he made both a fishing pole and a diamond mining tool?**

A: He reel-axed.

**Q: What do you get when you combine gravel, redstone, and a water block?**
A: Mud.

■

**Q: Why did Steve leave a bunch of butter in the Tundra Biome?**
A: He wanted cold, hard cash.

■

**Q: What did the tree say when it got tired of Steve trying to knock it down?**
A: "Leaf me alone!"

■

**Q: How did Steve know when the spawning was almost done?**
A: He used an egg-timer.

■

**Q: What's the most literate ore?**
A: Read-stone.

**Q: What happened to the glowstone when it got crushed?**

A: It was de-lighted.

■

**Q: What kind of stone is the least stable?**

A: Hobblestone.

■

**Q: Why can you get your sword stolen by another player?**

A: Because Minecraft is a cutthroat game.

■

**Q: What's the difference between a pro athlete and a Minecrafter?**

A: The Minecrafter doesn't mind getting sent to the bench.

■

**Q: Why are Minecrafters so healthy?**

A: Because they get their minerals every day.

**Q: What happened to Steve when he got his pickaxe stuck in his head?**

A: A splitting headache.

**Q: Are some swords better than others?**

A: Diamond Swords are a cut above the rest!

■

**Q: Why is glowstone so helpful when mining?**

A: It can really lighten your lord!

■

**Q: How is Minecraft like the Olympics?**

A: Everybody is after the metal.

■

**Q: Who makes all the sand in Minecraft?**

A: The sandman!

■

**Q: What happened when Steve's life meter fell?**

A: He had a heart attack.

# CHAPTER FIVE

## CAN YOU DIG IT (BY WHICH WE MEAN THESE TOTALLY RANDOM MINECRAFT JOKES)?

**Q: Why did Steve search for ore all day?**
A: Because he digs it.

■

**Q: How does Steve start a story?**
A: "Once upon a mine . . ."

■

**Q: What's a popular playground game in Minecraft?**
A: Crops and Robbers.

**Q: How can you tell if a Minecrafter has been playing with your cards?**

A: They've been shoveled.

■

**Q: Who's a Minecrafter's favorite president?**

A: William Howard Craft.

■

**Q: What's different about Christmas in Minecraft?**

A: Kids don't mind if Santa brings them Coal.

**Q: What's the only thing on Steve's "bucket list?"**

A: Lava. He's got to keep it somewhere!

■

**Q: What time of the year do Minecraft accountants work the hardest?**

A: Axe season.

■

**Q: Why couldn't Steve get in to see the R-rated movie?**

A: Because he's a miner.

■

**Q: What happened to Steve when an earthquake hit Overland while he was sleeping?**

A: It made his bedrock.

■

**Q: What would you get if you pushed a music box down a mineshaft?**

A: A flat miner.

**Q: What's cobblestone's favorite music?**
A: Rock music.

■

**Q: Why would a mushroom make a good roommate?**
A: It's a real fungi.

■

**Q: Where can you sell all your Minecraft eggs?**
A: At the spawn shop.

■

**Q: Why wasn't YouTube working for the ocelot?**
A: It turns out the video was on paws.

■

**Q: How are ocelots like potato chips?**
A: You can never have just one.

■

**Q: What did the pigman put on his rash?**
A: Oink-ment.

**Q: Why do Minecrafters use horses?**
A: They're a very stable animal.

■

**Q: What did the teacher say to the curious jungle cat?**
A: "You sure do ocelot of questions."

■

**Q: Why did Steve need mouthwash after killing a passive mob?**
A: Because he had bat breath.

■

**Q: What does a Minecraft turkey say?**
A: Cobble, cobble, cobble!

■

**Q: Why are cows so much trouble for miners?**
A: They play herd to get.

■

**Q: Why is Steve's horse so loyal?**
A: He used to serve in the neeeeeeigh-vy.

**Q: Did you hear about the pile of kittens that spawned?**
A: It was a meow-ntain.

■

**Q: Why did the chicken cross the road?**
A: Because there aren't any cars in Minecraft.

■

**Q: How do you keep a pig from getting in your house?**
A: Leave the door open.

■

**Q: What happened to the guy who fell into the void?**
A: Nothing! He double-tapped space.

■

**Q: Why is Minecraft so popular?**
A: People really dig the interface.

■

**Q: What Minecraft creature do you need to start a baseball game?**
A: Bats.

**Q: How many cats can you spawn in Minecraft?**
A: Ocelots and ocelots.

■

**Q: Did you hear about the mean Minecrafter?**
A: He was rotten to the ore.

■

**Q: What happened to Steve when a ball landed on his face?**
A: It poked his eye out.

■

**Q: What do you get when you cross a cow and a mushroom?**
A: A Mooshroom.

■

**Q: What did Steve do after a fight with Alex?**
A: He ore-pologized.

**Q: What kind of snake would you find in Minecraft?**

A: A boa constructor.

**Q: If it looks like a duck and sounds like a duck, what is it?**

A: A chicken in Minecraft.

■

**Q: What do you call cheese you find in Minecraft?**

A: Notch yo cheese.

**Q: What happened to the sheep that stepped on a flower?**

A: It dyed.

■

**Q: How do you make a tree float?**

A: Put it in root beer.

■

**Q: Why did the chicken cross the road?**

A: Because the player kept hitting him for feathers.

■

**Q: Why do Minecraft bunnies jump around so much?**

A: They're hoppy to see you.

**Q: What do you call a grumpy cow?**
A: Mooooody.

■

**Q: What should you say to a slow cow?**
A: Mooooooove it!

■

**Q: Why did Steve take home all twelve bunnies he found?**
A: He didn't want to split hares.

■

**Q: Why do Minecraft chickens have flat feet?**
A: To stamp out the forest fires.

■

**Q: Why do Minecraft cows have flat feet?**
A: To stamp out the flaming chickens.

■

**Q: When's the best time to go looking for cows?**
A: During the moooonlight.

**Q: What did Steve think when the sheep spawned with pink wool?**

A: He thought he'd dyed.

■

**Q: What did Steve's mom tell him to do when he was a boy?**

A: "Mine your manners!"

■

**Q: What else did Steve's mom tell him when he was a boy?**

A: "Sticks and stones may break your bones, but so will tiny magma cubes, and creepers, and zombies, and skeletons . . ."

■

**Q: Steve's chest was full, but he couldn't use anything inside of it. Why?**

A: Because a cat was sitting on top of it.

■

**Q: What city would a Minecrafter want to visit?**

A: Flint, Michigan.

**Q: What other city would a Minecrafter most want to visit?**
A: Mine-eapolis.

■

**Q: Why was the man trying to dig to the center of the Earth?**
A: Because he had never heard of Minecraft.

■

**Q: What does Steve do with a door?**
A: Steve leaves.

■

**Q: What falls off of Steve's trees into Steve's yard?**
A: Steve's leaves.

■

**Q: What does Steve do with a butcher's knife?**
A: Steve cleaves.

**Q: What does Steve call annoyances like hostile mobs and unplanned explosions?**

A: Steve's peeves.

■

**Q: What does Steve do when all his livestock dies?**

A: Steve grieves.

■

**Q: What does Steve do when he eats too much cake?**

A: Steve heaves.

■

Three of the most popular basketball teams in Minecraft: The Denver Golden Nuggets, the Detroit Pistons, and the Portland Trail Blaze.

■

**Q: Who's the biggest superhero in Minecraft?**

A: Spawn.

**Q: Who's the other biggest superhero in Minecraft?**
A: Iron Man.

■

**Q: Why did the villagers respect the towers of obsidian?**
A: Because they were pillars of the community.

■

**Q: What Pokémon would fit well into Minecraft?**
A: Diglett.

■

**Q: Why did the villager cross the road?**
A: To reach the village.

■

**Q: What did the cranky villager baby say to his mom?**
A: "You won't be able to tell me what to do in twenty minutes when I'm all grown up!"

■

**Q: What did Steve say to a villager?**
A: "It's rude to stare!"

**Q: What does Steve do for good luck before mining?**
A: He knocks on wood.

■

**Q: Why do teenagers love Minecraft?**
A: They love to hang out on corners.

■

**Q: Why did Steve want to visit Ireland?**
A: Because he heard it's the Emerald Isle.

■

**Q: What kind of money seems to just float away?**
A: Butter-flies.

■

**Q: What kind of TV does Steve watch?**
A: A Sand-sung.

■

**Q: What do you get when you punch a tree?**
A: A broken hand, unless you're playing Minecraft.

**Q: What did Steve do when he found iron ore instead of diamonds?**
A: He was minerly disappointed.

■

**Q: Why did Steve build a house in the Extreme Hills?**
A: To see what it felt like to live on the edge.

■

**Q: Why can't trees knit you a wool sweater?**
A: Because they're always dropping their needles.

■

**Q: What should you do if you get stuck in the Tundra Biome?**
A: Just chill.

■

**Q: In what country is Minecraft popular?**
A: E-stone-ia.

■

**Q: Who are the best singers in Minecraft?**
A: Chorus flowers.

**Q: What happens when pirates hit Minecraft?**

A: They store all the orrrrrrrre.

■

**Q: How come some things last in Minecraft and others don't?**

A: It's just Notch-ural selection.

■

**Q: What did Steve's mom tell him?**

A: "You're the Golden Apple of my eye."

■

**Q: Why can't you play hide-and-seek in the Mountain Biome?**

A: Because the mountains are always peaking.

■

**Q: Why did Steve add trees to his house?**

A: He wanted to spruce up the place.

**Q: Can you make a porcupine in Minecraft?**
A: No, but you can cross a cactus and a tree and get a pokey-pine!

■

**Q: What was in the bouquet Steve got for Alex?**
A: Redstone roses, butter-cups, and mari-golds.

■

**Q: What's a Minecrafter's favorite card game?**
A: Hearts.

■

**Q: Why did the tree move biomes?**
A: It wanted to branch out.

■

**Q: Why is the Mountain Biome good for singing?**
A: Because it's got great range.

■

**Q: What inventor would make a good Minecrafter?**
A: George Washington Carver.

**Q: Why do so many villagers go into farming?**
A: Because the field is growing.

■

**Q: Did you hear about Steve's pet chicken?**
A: It was a personal fowl.

■

**Q: Why was there gold in the dirt field?**
A: It was rich soil.

■

**Q: How do spawn hatch?**
A: They look for the eggs-it.

■

**Q: What state would a Minecrafter not want to visit?**
A: Ore-gone.

**Q: What does Steve think about when he's feeling philosophical?**

A: Which spawned first: the chicken or the egg?

**Q: Why did Steve not feel like building one day?**
A: He didn't have the hearts.

■

**Q: Why should you never tell a joke to a spawning egg?**
A: So it won't crack up.

■

**Q: How do Minecrafters clean their faces?**
A: With coal cream.

■

**Q: Do hipsters like Minecraft?**
A: Yeah, man, they dig it.

# CHAPTER 6

## SONGS FOR MINECRAFTING

"We Are Nether Nether Getting Back Together"

■

"Ready Ore Not"

■

"Wild Horses"

■

"We Will Block You"

■

"Block This Town"

■

"Block the Casbah"

"Hip to Be Square"

■

"Diamond's Are a Miner's Best Friend"

■

"Sweet Child O' Mine"

■

"Gold Digger"

■

"Ore Than a Feeling"

■

"All Along the Notchtower"

■

"Shovel Me What You Got"

■

"A Hole New World"

"Every Day I'm Shovelin'"

■

"Lost in My Potions"

■

"Nether Say Nether"

■

"Nether My Love"

■

"Get Blocky"

■

"Block Be a Lady Tonight"

■

"Steve of Destruction"

■

"At Long Blast Love"

"At Blast"

■

"Welcome to the Jungle Biome"

■

"You Dropped a Bomb On Me"

"Lookin' for Lava in All the Wrong Places"

"She's Crafty"

■

"Ghast Dance"

■

"Block on the Wild Side"

■

"Block On"

■

"Block Like an Egyptian"

"Walking On Broken Ghast"

■

"Digging Your Scene"

■

"Ghast Car"

■

"Life in the Blast Lane"

■

"Classical Ghast"

■

"Ghastbusters"

■

"Witchy Woman"

■

"Witchcraft"

"Steves in the Temple"

■

"Gypsies, Tramps, and Steves"

■

"Go Ask Alex"

■

"All Things Must Blast"

■

"Block Rockin' Beats"

■

"Rock Around the Block"

■

"Frere Blocka"

■

"Sittin' on the Block of the Bay"

"Everybody's Blockin'"

■

"Something to Block About"

■

"Sweet Blockin' Woman"

■

"Block That Block"

■

"Blocking in Your Sleep"

■

"Mine Games"

■

"Always on My Mine"

■

"Free Your Mine"

"Suspicious Mines"

■

"Blocking with a Ghast"

■

"Blockin' After Midnight"

■

"It's a Hard Block Life"

■

"Make 'Em Craft"

■

"Diamond Girl"

■

"Mr. Mojangles"

■

"Do You Want To Build (Anything Other Than a Snowman)?"

"Turn to Redstone"

■

"Sword Up!"

■

"Swords Get in the Way"

■

"Toccata and Fugue in D Miner" by Johann Sebastian Block

■

"Ring of Fireballs"

■

"Weakness Potion No. 9"

■

"Let Me Blow Your Mine"

"Do You Want to Build a Snow Golem?"

"The Square of Life"

■

"Baby, It's Coaled Outside"

■

"Man in the Box"

"Jumpin' Jack Flash is a Ghast Ghast Ghast"

■

"Blaze of Glory"

■

"Nether Gonna Give You Up"

■

"Don't Fear the Creeper"

■

"Don't Fence Me In"

■

"Maxwell's Silver Hammer"

■

"Another Brick in the Wall"

■

"Build Me Up, Buttercup"

"Heart of Ghast"

■

"Digging in the Dirt"

■

"In By Boom"

■

"Fields of Gold"

■

"The End"

■

"Light My Fire"

■

"There is a Torch That Never Goes Out"

■

"Shine On You Crazy Diamond Pickaxe"

"A Nether Day in Paradise"

■

"Brick House"

■

"TNT (Dynamite)"

■

"Under the Bedrock"

■

"Season of the Witch"

■

"The Night Time is the Right Time"

■

"Down on the Corner"

■

"Let's Get it Carted"

"Mr. Sandman"

■

"Desert Biome Rose"

■

"Like a Rock"

■

"Big Rock Candy Mountain Biome"

■

"We Built This City"

■

"Shields of Gold"

■

"Journey to the Center of the Mine"

■

"Jenny From the Block"

"Follow the Yellow Brick Road"

■

"The Boxer"

# CHAPTER 7

## BLOCK-BLOCK, WHO'S THERE?

Knock-knock.

Who's there?

Cow.

Cow who?

Cow are you today?

■

Knock-knock.

Who's there?

Notch.

Notch who?

It you're making nachos, hold the jalapeños.

■

Knock-knock.

Who's there?

Notch.

Notch who?

You're Notch going to let me in, are you?

■

Knock-knock.

Who's there?

Notch.

Notch who?

Gesundheit!

■

Knock-knock.

Who's there?

Notch.

Notch who?

Notch me!

■

Knock-knock.

Who's there?

Water.

Water who?

Water you waiting for?

■

Knock-knock.

Who's there?

Leaf.

Leaf who?

Leaf me alone!

Hey, you're the one knocking. You leaf *me* alone!

■

Knock-knock.

Who's there?

Wood.

Wood who?

Wooden you like to know!

■

Knock-knock.

Who's there?

Coal.

Coal who?

It's Coal out here! Let me in!

■

Knock-knock.

Who's there?

Hoe.

Hoe who?

Hoe did you know it was me?

■

Knock-knock.

Who's there?

Aloha.

Aloha who?

Aloha myself into the mineshaft.

■

Knock-knock.

Who's there?

Blast.

Blast who?

This is your blast chance!

■

Knock-knock.

Who's there?

Confused pig.

Confused pig who?

Moo!

■

Knock-knock.

Who's there?

Spell block.

Spell block who?

B-L-O-C-K-W-H-O.

■

Knock-knock.

Who's there?

Sword.

Sword who?

Sword your inventory, it's a mess!

■

Knock-knock.

Who's there?

A boat.

A boat who?

A boat time I got here.

■

Knock-knock.

Who's there?

Sword.

Sword who?

Sword of a stupid question.

■

Knock-knock.

Who's there?

*Aab Aab!*

Get out of here, backward Sheep!

■

Knock-knock.

Who's there?

Ocelot.

Ocelot who?

(Ocelot runs away.)

■

Knock-knock.

Who's there?

Ocelot.

Ocelot who?

Ocelot of questions. Let me in!

■

Knock-knock.

Who's there?

Dog.

Dog who?

Doggone it, open the door, there's a ghast after me!

Knock-knock.

Who's there?

Esther.

Esther who?

Esther a cave spider behind you?

■

Knock-knock.

Who's there?

Eileen.

Eileen who?

Eileen'd on a wall too hard and it collapsed!

■

Knock-knock.

Who's there?

Philip.

Philip who?

Philip my chest with diamonds, please!

■

Knock-knock

Who's there?

Piglet.

Piglet who?

Piglet me in the last time I was here.

■

Knock-knock.

Who's there?

Cows go.

Cows go who?

No, cows go moo.

■

Knock-knock.

Who's there?

Figs.

Figs who?

Fix your fence!

■

Knock-knock.

Who's there?

Farmer.

Farmer who?

Farmer distance, your house looks much larger.

■

Knock-knock.

Who's there?

Diamond ore.

WOW, WHERE??

■

Knock-knock.

Who's there?

Stick.

Stick who?

Stick around.

■

Knock-knock.

Who's there?

Fire.

Fire who?

Fire! Get me an axe and a bucket of water!

■

Knock-knock.

Who's there?

Armor.

Armor who?

Armor crops okay?

■

Knock-knock.

Who's there?

Tunnel.

Tunnel who?

Tunnel mobs will spawn if we don't get some torches soon!

■

Knock-knock.

Who's there?

House.

House who?

House am I supposed to build this all by myself?

■

Knock-knock.

Who's there?

Chest.

Chest who?

Chest got back from a mineshaft. I need a place to store my loot.

Knock-knock.

Who's there?

Disappearing pickaxe.

Disappearing pickaxe who?

No fair, I got here so fast!

■

Knock-knock.

Who's there?

Island.

Island who?

Island in the water, but I still take damage!

■

Knock-knock.

Who's there?

Snow.

Snow who?

Snow place like home in the Tundra Biome!

■

Knock-knock.

Who's there?

Villager.

Villager who?

Villager home, villager chests!

■

Knock-knock.

Who's there?

Orange.

Orange who?

Orange you going to help me dig?

Knock-knock.

Who's there?

Block.

Block who?

Block that guy, he's a griefer!

■

Knock-knock.

Who's there?

TNT.

TNT who?

Hey, I didn't know you could yodel!

■

Knock-knock.

Who's there?

Block.

Block who?

Block this way.

■

Knock-knock.

Who's there?

Dye.

Dye who?

Dye the wool!

■

Knock-knock.

Who's there?

Arrow.

Arrow who?

Arrow on the side of caution.

■

Knock-knock.

Who's there?

Marsh.

Marsh who?

Marsh on out here!

■

Knock-knock.

Who's there?

Oak.

Oak who?

Oak out below!

■

Knock-knock.

Who's there?

Gravel.

Gravel who?

Gravel everywhere! Get out before you suffocate!

■

Knock-knock.

Who's there?

House.

House who?

House you doing?

■

Knock-knock.

Who's there?

Pixel.

Pixel who?

Pixel this.

■

Knock-knock.

Who's there?

Wool.

Wool who?

Wool you let me in?

■

Knock-knock.

Who's there?

Cart.

Cart who.

I can feel my cart pounding!

■

Knock-knock.

Who's there?

Cactus.

Cactus who?

Quick, get a cactus ball!

■

Knock-knock.

Who's there?

Diamond.

Diamond who?

You're diamond me crazy!

■

Knock-knock.

Who's there?

Brew.

Brew who?

Hey, don't cry!

■

Knock-knock.

Who's there?

Seed.

Seed who?

Seed what I did there?

■

Knock-knock.

Who's there?

Can't torch.

Can't torch who?

Can't torch this!

■

Knock-knock.

Who's there?

Gunpowder.

Gunpowder who?

Gunpowder my nose.

■

Knock-knock.

Who's there?

Water.

Water who?

Water you talking about?

■

Knock-knock.

Who's there?

Ore.

Ore who?

Ore else!

■

Knock-knock.

Who's there?

Canoe who?

Canoe come out and fix my cart?

■

Knock-knock.

Who's there?

Dino.

Dino who?

Dino-mite!

■

Knock-knock.

Who's there?

Aida.

Aida who?

Aida lot of golden apples and now I've got tummy ache!

■

Knock-knock.

Who's there?

Ash.

Ash who?

Bless you. I did not mean to make you sneeze!

■

Knock-knock.

Who's there?

Barry.

Barry who?

Barry the treasure where no one will find it.

■

Knock-knock.

Who's there?

Noah.

Noah who?

Noah good place to dig?

■

Knock-knock.

Who's there?

Waiter.

Waiter who?

Waiter I get my hands on some emeralds!

■

Knock-knock.

Who's there?

Armor.

Armor who?

Armor people in there or is it just you?

■

Knock-knock.

Who's there?

Egg.

Egg who?

Egg-cited to spawn!

■

Knock-knock.

Who's there?

Spider.

Spider who?

Spider what everyone says, I like you!

■

Knock-knock.

Who's there?

Everest.

Everest who?

Do we Everest from building stuff?

■

Knock-knock.

Who's there?

Brick.

Brick who?

Brick or treat!

■

Knock-knock

Who's there?

Oliver.

Oliver who?

Oliver crops are getting snatched!

■

Knock-knock.

Who's there?

Macon.

Macon who?

Forget it, I'll be, Macon my own house!

■

Knock-knock.

Who's there?

Anita.

Anita who?

Anita borrow a shovel, quick!

■

Knock-knock.

Who's there?

Max.

Max who?

Max life meter!

■

Knock-knock.

Who's there?

Butter.

Butter who?

Butter not touch my inventory!

■

Knock-knock.

Who's there?

Wayne.

Wayne who?

The Wayne is really coming down, let's go fishing!

■

Knock-knock.

Who's there?

Raymond.

Raymond who?

Raymond me later to put up a lava moat around the house.

■

Knock-knock.

Who's there?

Hannah.

Hannah who?

Hannah some of those golden apples, I'm starving!

■

Knock-knock.

Who's there?

Mia.

Mia who?

Mia hand is killing me from punching trees all day!

■

Knock-knock.

Who's there?

Anna.

Anna who?

Anna chance you're up for a trade?

■

Knock-knock.

Who's there?

Chest?

Chest who?

Chest checking in!

■

Knock-knock.

Who's there?

Iran.

Iran who?

Iran from a hostile mob, open up!

■

Knock-knock.

Come on in. There are no locks on the doors anyway.

■

Knock-knock.

Not now, I'm playing Minecraft!

# CHAPTER 8

## SWIFTLY, STEVE!

"I haven't caught a fish all day," Steve said without debate.

■

"I need to sharpen my pickaxe," said Steve bluntly.

■

"I punched that tree three times," said Steve triumphantly.

■

"I only like wheat bread," Steve said wryly.

■

"I should've brought a jacket to the Ice Biome," Steve said coldly.

■

"They pulled the wool over my eyes," Steve said sheepishly.

"The boat is leaking," Steve said balefully.

■

"That creeper exploded so hard smoke is coming off of it," Steve fumed.

"I've only got five left on my life meter," Steve said half-heartedly.

■

"It sure did get to be dawn soon," Steve mourned.

■

"Someone should be at the door soon," Steve guessed.

■

"I need a work animal to help me out," Steve said hoarsely.

■

"Blow on the fire so it doesn't go out," Steve bellowed.

■

"Come on in to my new house," Steve admitted.

■

"There are only two witches instead of three," Steve recounted.

■

"I've never crashed my cart," said Steve recklessly.

"That's the last time I try to touch a zombie," said Steve offhandedly.

■

"That used to be my diamond mine," Steve exclaimed.

■

"Measure twice before you build," Steve remarked.

■

"I'm not afraid of the dark," Steve said delightedly.

■

"I had to return from the sea," Steve reported.

■

"Okay you can borrow my hoe again," Steve relented.

■

"This oar is broken," said Steve robustly.

"Please don't point that arrow at me," said Steve, quivering.

"I love red ones better than green ones," said Steve, applauding.

■

"I only have enough planks to go up halfway," said Steve with a blank stare.

"Stop, horse!" cried Steve woefully.

■

"I swear this house is taller than it was yesterday," said Steve gruesomely.

■

"Watch what my sword can do," said Steve cuttingly.

■

"I can't remember what I built yesterday," said Steve lackadaisically.

■

"Shall we look for the coldest of the golems?" Steve asked icily.

■

"You've got to make a house plan somewhere," Steve ruled.

■

"That's a huge squid!" said Steve superficially.

"Now I have the tools to chop down that tree," said Steve with a heavy accent.

■

"I've dug all the way into the bedrock," Steve said, bored.

■

"Rowing hurts my hands," said Steve callously.

■

"I've got to stop this motor," Steve choked.

■

"I just came in through the door," said Steve, entranced.

■

"Has anyone seen my blue trousers?" asked Steve expansively.

■

"I'm falling into a void," said Steve, his voice falling.

■

"I just got done smelting some tools," Steve said ironically.

"I'm halfway up a mountain," Steve alleged.

■

"Don't add too much water to that recipe," said Steve with great concentration.

■

"Would you like to buy some raw salmon?" asked Steve selfishly.

■

"I have three houses, and I'm going to build another," said Steve forebodingly.

■

"I've got sand in my dinner," said Steve grittily.

■

"I have to keep these eggs warm," Steve said honestly.

■

"I've run out of wool," said Steve, knitting his brow.

"Let's punch down some trees!" said Steve, lumbering.

■

"The zombies got Alex!" said Steve mistakenly.

■

"The door's ajar," said Steve openly.

■

"I swallowed some of the glass from that broken window," Steve said painfully.

■

"I've removed all the feathers from this chicken," said Steve pluckily.

■

"That ocelot sounds happy now she's been fed," said Steve purposefully.

"Eating glowstone makes me feel funny," said Steve radiantly.

■

"I deal with creepers every seven days," said Steve weakly.

■

"We can use a water solution," Steve acquiesced.

■

"Check out the winding staircase I built," said Steve coyly.

■

"You've got to be egging me on," yolked Steve.

■

"I hate creepers but they sure are a pretty shade of green," said Steve jadedly.

"Fire!" yelled Steve alarmingly.

"I've got to fix my cart," said Steve mechanically.

■

"I just put up some steel supports!" Steve beamed.

■

"Check out my new chicken!" clucked Steve.

"I'm carrying too much ore," said Steve heavily.

■

"The squid died!" Steve wailed blubberingly.

■

"I'll take those diamonds then," said Steve appropriately.

■

"Yes, I was in the coop when it exploded," admitted Steve, with egg on his face.

■

"That skeleton better leave my knees alone," said Steve arrowgantly.

■

"The exit is right over there," Steve pointed out.

"My pickaxe is dull," said Steve pointlessly.

■

"Creepers are coming, so I'm out of here," said Steve believingly.

■

"All my crops have died," said Steve witheringly.

■

"All I ever do is milk this cow," Steve uttered continuously.

■

"I think my roof is about to collapse," Steve upheld.

■

"These emeralds are worth more every day," said Steve appreciatively.

"I hope I don't run into any skeletons," said Steve gravely.

"I think I just swallowed a fishing lure," said Steve with baited breath.

■

"I must be tired from running away from mobs all night," Steve worked out.

■

"Of course I can make armor out of chains," Steve replied by mail.

"Oh, this isn't a diamond at all," said Steve stonily.

■

"This has been a grave undertaking," said Steve cryptically.

■

"Things are always happening to me," said Steve incidentally.

■

"I've run out of wool," said Steve, knitting his brow.

■

"I think I need more wood," Steve opined.

■

"Never pound anything into glass," said Steve painstakingly.

■

"Who stabbed me with their pickaxe?" asked Steve pointedly.

"I don't want this sweet potato," Steve yammered.

■

"I teleported right out of there," said the Enderman, visibly moved.

# CHAPTER 9

## STEVE WALKS INTO A MINESHAFT

Steve walks into a mineshaft and drops his sandwich into the giant hole. He lost his lunch.

■

A horse wanders into a village. The villager asks, "Hey, why the long face?"

■

A zombie and a skeleton walk into a restaurant. The waiter says to the skeleton, "You're gutless," and then says to the zombie, "You're dead meat!"

A villager walks into a café. The waiter asks, "Hey, why the long nose?"

■

Steve and Alex walk into a café. The waiter says, "Please leave. We don't serve miners."

A spider, a skeleton, and a zombie walk into a bar. The spider gets stuck on it, and the skeleton and the zombie take suffocation damage.

■

A creeper walks into a restaurant, and the waiter says, "Get out of here. Last time you blew up for no reason!"

■

A spider walks into a restaurant. The waiter says, "You can't come in. Last night you got so crazy that you were climbing the walls!"

■

A creeper, a zombie, and a skeleton walk into a house. They wreck the place that took weeks to build.

■

A chicken walks into a building. That's the end of the joke.

A zombie goes into work. His boss asks, "Did you sleep last night? You look a little bit dead."

■

A creeper walks into a restaurant. That's the end of the joke.

Two creepers walk into a house. One says to the other, "I'm going to go outsssside for sssssome fresh air." The other creeper says, "Just wait two sssseconds, and we'll both be outsssside."

■

One creeper walks up to another creeper and says, "Hello." The second creeper says, "Wow, a talking creeper!"

■

Three miners walk up to a workbench. The first miner says, "What a day! After all those zombies, I need a new sword." The second miner says, "That's nothing. I used up all my arrows killing creepers. They ever even saw it coming." The third miner says, "Ssssss…"

■

A skeleton, a creeper, and Steve walk into a building. Steve walks out with a broken record.

■

Steve walks into a party and sees that the only other three guests are skeletons. "Boy," he says, "it's dead in here."

Steve and a blaze go to the park and play a game of tag. The blaze tagged Steve, Steve catches on fire, and the blaze runs away. That was the ender the game.

■

A pig walks into a café. The manager says, "Sorry we don't serve food here."

■

A creeper and a zombie walk into a bar. The zombie leaves in pieces.

■

A zombie, a skeleton, and a creeper jump out of a crashing airplane. The skeleton jumps without a parachute, and figures he'll just put himself together after he hits the ground. The zombie wears a parachute to protect his delicate, rotting flesh. The creeper just blows up and figures he'll respawn later.

A skeleton walks into a café. He orders a glass of water and a mop.

■

A ghast walks into a café. "What can I get you?" the barista asked. "Nothing," the ghast says. "It'll go right through me."

■

A mushroom walks into an ice cream shop and buys for everyone in line. A villager says to the mushroom, "Wow, what a fun guy!"

■

A tree walks into a store. "Who's that?" one clerk asks the other. "I don't know," says the other clerk, "but I hear he's a very shady character."

■

A blaze walks into a café. The waiter says, "You can come in, but don't get everybody fired up!"

Steve walks into a café, orders a coffee, and then goes outside, climbs up on the roof, and places the drink up there. When he comes back inside, the barista asks, “Why did you do that?” Steve replies, “This one is on the house.”

■

A creeper walks into a restaurant. And then he immediately runs out. The creeper didn’t know it was an ocelot place.

■

Two witches walk into a restaurant. “Have you seen our third?” asked one witch. “Well,” asked the manager, “what did she look like?”

■

A creeper walks into a village. Everyone freaks out. “Don’t worry,” said the creeper. “I’m armless.”

■

A horse walks into a restaurant. The waiter says, “Hey.” The horse asks, “How did you know that’s what I was going to order?”

Steve walks to a restaurant with a bucket of lava. "Raw meat," he orders. "I'll heat it up myself, thanks."

■

A witch covered in sandstone walks into a deli. The worker says, "Hey we have a menu item named after you!" The witch replies, "You have a menu item named Karen?"

■

An Enderman asks to use the restroom. "Sure," says the manager, "it's just down the stares."

■

A spider walks up to a spider jockey. "Need a ride?" the spider asks. "No thanks," replies the spider jockey. "What are you," the spider replied, "chicken?" "No," said the jockey. "I'm a skeleton."

■

A skeleton walks into a smoothie shop. "What'll it be?" asks the worker. "Anything," replies the skeleton. "I'm bone dry."

■

A zombie and a skeleton walk into a restaurant and ask to sit outside. They instantly burn.

# EXTRA

## CRAFT AN ANSWER TO THESE *MINECRAFT* RIDDLES

■

**Q: Why is an adult Minecrafter still like a kid?**

A: Because he's a miner.

**Q: What roars but doesn't have a mouth?**

A: A firey explosion!

■

**Q: What's the best way to talk to a hostile mob?**

A: From far away.

**Q: What's the capital of Minecraft?**
A: M.

■

**Q: How is Minecraft like golf?**
A: There are woods, irons, sand, and too many holes.

■

**Q: What do you call a ghast in the Taiga Biome?**
A: Lost!

■

**Q: Where are King Solomon's mines?**
A: In King Solomon's Minecraft.

■

**Q: What falls every day but never hits the ground?**
A: Night.

■

**Q: What Minecraft item is brown and sticky?**
A: A stick.

**Q: What do you find in the middle of a biome?**
A: The letter "O."

■

**Q: What did Steve wear to the dance?**
A: A green shirt and blue pants!

■

**Q: Where did chickens first spawn?**
A: Chick-ago.

■

**Q: Why did the chicken cross the road?**
A: Trick question. There are no roads in Minecraft!

**Q: If you're tired, what biome do you need to go to?**
A: For-rest.

■

**Q: Why does Minecraft make everyone selfish?**
A: Because it's makes people say, "mine, mine, mine!"

■

**Q: Why did Steve try to pick up an entire baseball field?**
A: Because it was a huge diamond!

■

**Q: When is The End just the beginning?**
A: When you're playing Minecraft.

■

**Q: You wake up on a small island. There's no land in sight for miles, and there are no trees. How do you survive?**
A: Create a new world.

# CHATPER TEN

## THE MINECRAFT CAFÉ

**Entrees**

Craft Macaroni and Cheese

Rice Creepies

Build-your-own omelets

Steak, Well-Enderized

Boxed Lunch

Pop-Tarts

Wood Plank-Grilled Rockfish

Rabbit Toast

Swordfish

Arrows con Pollo

Quick-Cook Bacon

Mushroom Soup

Armor Hot Dogs

Sushi

TNT-Explosion-Smoked Salmon

Steak Tartare (raw meat with an egg on top)

Smelt

**Side Items**

Popcorn with "I Can't Believe It's Not Butter"

Square Watermelons

Blaze-cooked Sweet Potatoes

Bouillon Cubes

Stonefruit

Golden Apples

Blue Diamond Almonds

Chips

**Desserts**

Creeps Suzette

Ghastly Boo-Berry Pie

Donut Holes

Cactus Candy

Marshmallow Creeps

Cobbler

Oreos

Snowballs

Redstone Currants

Stone Scones

Rocky Road Ice Cream

Spider Eye Pie

Rock Candy

Butter Brickle Ice Cream

Dirt Cake with Butter-Cream Frosting

Sugar Cubes

**Drinks**

Coal-a

Ore-ange Juice

Tree Punch

Builders Tea

Mintcraft Tea

Hole Milk

Water Blocks

■

**Q: What's the problem with a mycelium build?**
A: There's too mush-room.

■

**Q: Why didn't Steve have any energy to mine?**
A: He was on a low-carve diet.

■

**Q: What goes great with Minecraft bacon?**
A: Monster eggs.

■

**Q: What did Steve bring to the cookout?**
A: The coals.

**Q: What would you get if you fed a bunch of diamonds to a cow?**

A: Blue cheese.

■

**Q: Why didn't Steve want any clownfish?**

A: It tasted funny.

■

**Q: What kind of cake is hard as stone?**

A: Marble cake.

**Q: How can you tell if a chicken is rotten?**
A: It lays deviled eggs.

■

**Q: What do playing Minecraft and dessert have in common?**
A: They're both a piece of cake.

■

**Q: What kind of vegetables grow in the cold biomes?**
A: Snow peas.

■

**Q: Where does Steve buy organic vegetables?**
A: Hole Foods.

■

**Q: How are peaches like Minecraft?**
A: They're full of pits.

**Q: How is Swiss cheese like Minecraft?**
A: It's full of holes.

■

**Q: What do you get when you cross an anvil with some golden apples?**
A: Applesauce.

■

**Q: What can you eat during a cart ride?**
A: Fast food.

■

**Q: What did Steve do when he was in a jam?**
A: Luckily, he had some bread.

■

**Q: How did the spawn egg cross the road?**
A: It scrambled.

**Q: Why did the rabbit steal Steve's gold?**

A: Because it was 14-carrots.

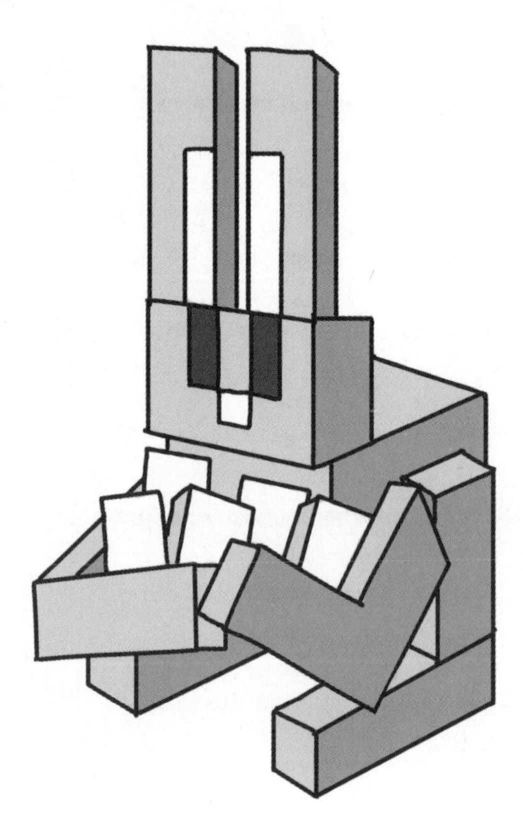

**Q: What's the most fun crop to grow in Minecraft?**

A: Wheeeeeeeeeat!

■

**Q: What's the sweetest of all biomes?**

A: Desert.